MN

W9-AXZ-079

Great Artists
Frederic Remington

ABDO
Publishing Company

Joanne Mattern

visit us at
www.abdopub.com

Published by ABDO Publishing Company, 4940 Viking Drive, Edina, Minnesota 55435.
Copyright © 2005 by Abdo Consulting Group, Inc. International copyrights reserved in all
countries. No part of this book may be reproduced in any form without written permission from
the publisher. The Checkerboard Library™ is a trademark and logo of ABDO Publishing
Company.

Printed in the United States.

Cover Photo: Frederic Remington Art Museum
Interior Photos: Corbis pp. 5, 13, 15, 17, 19, 21, 27, 29; Frederic Remington Art Museum pp. 1,
     9, 10, 11, 25, 28; Getty Images pp. 21, 23

Series Coordinator: Megan Murphy
Editors: Jennifer R. Krueger, Megan Murphy
Cover Design: Neil Klinepier
Interior Design: Dave Bullen

Library of Congress Cataloging-in-Publication Data

Mattern, Joanne, 1963-
     Frederic Remington / Joanne Mattern.
        p. cm. -- (Great artists)
     Includes index.
     ISBN 1-59197-848-3
     1. Remington, Frederic, 1861-1909--Juvenile literature. 2. Artists--United States--
Biography--Juvenile literature. 3. West (U.S.)--In art--Juvenile literature. I. Title.

N6537.R4M38 2005
709'.2--dc22
[B]
                                                                            2004052810

Contents

Remington

Frederic Remington is a famous American artist. He lived from 1861 to 1909. As a magazine illustrator, he created many drawings and paintings of the American West. He was also a sculptor. Remington was known for his work as a war artist as well.

Remington lived most of his life in the eastern United States. But, he painted a very different place. Most of Remington's work focuses on images of the American West. His pictures show an exciting world of life on the plains. He painted cowboys, Native Americans, soldiers, and horses.

Remington loved the West. He made many trips to Arizona, Texas, and New Mexico in his lifetime. His realistic work illustrates the stories of the people who lived in the West during this time. Remington's art made this rugged land come to life.

Frederic Sackrider Remington

1861 ~ Frederic Sackrider Remington was born on October 4; his father left to serve in the Civil War two months after he was born.

1875 ~ Remington went to military school in Vermont.

1878 ~ Remington attended the Yale School of the Fine Arts.

1880 ~ Remington's father died.

1881 ~ Remington headed West for the first time.

1884 ~ Remington moved to Kansas City, Missouri; his new wife, Eva, joined him but only stayed three months.

1885 ~ Remington attended the Art Students League in New York City; within a year, he established himself as a magazine illustrator.

1895 ~ Remington sculpted *The Bronco Buster*.

1905 ~ Remington began modeling *The Big Cowboy*.

1907 and 1908 ~ Remington burned many of his paintings.

1909 ~ Remington died on December 26.

- Frederic Remington illustrated more than 100 articles in his lifetime.

- Remington loved pranks and often got into trouble. As a young boy, he tormented a schoolgirl by painting her cat green.

- Remington's father's family was extremely wealthy. Despite Remington's carelessness with his finances, his Uncle Bill helped him with money throughout his life.

- Remington traveled extensively throughout his life. He visited Canada, Germany, Russia, and North Africa as a correspondent and artist. He made many trips out West over the years as well.

- By 1887, Remington had progressed from pen and ink drawings to oil and watercolor paintings.

- In 1895, Remington published his first book of illustrations called *Pony Tracks*.

Son of a Soldier

Frederic Sackrider Remington was born in Canton, New York, on October 4, 1861. Canton is a small village in northern New York State. Frederic was the only child of Seth and Clara Remington.

Seth Remington owned a newspaper called the *Plaindealer*. At the time, the United States was fighting the **Civil War**. When Frederic was only two months old, his father sold the newspaper. Then, he left to join the Union army.

Frederic's father returned home when the war ended in 1865. He had been a colonel in the war and was honored for bravery. As a war hero, he was very popular in Canton. So, Frederic received special treatment because he was Seth's son. He became spoiled from the attention.

Seth repurchased the *Plaindealer* in 1867. However, the newspaper plant burned down three years later. Seth soon found work in Ogdensburg, New York. The family moved there in 1873. At this time, Seth also began raising and racing horses.

*Canton, New York,
in the 1870s*

Military School

Growing up, Frederic did not like school. He thought schoolwork was boring and often skipped his lessons. Frederic preferred to spend time outdoors instead. He loved to camp, fish, and hunt. He played rough and often teased his schoolmates.

Seth wanted Frederic to go to school to be an army officer. So, Frederic's parents sent him to a military school in Vermont when he was 13. Seth hoped military school would help Frederic get better grades. He also hoped it would make a military career more appealing to his son.

Remington in his
military school uniform

Remington kept a diary for most of his life. Many of his journal sketches have a military theme, such as these from his later years.

But, Frederic hated military school. He was not used to following strict rules. He was also not used to being **disciplined** when he did something wrong. His studies bored him, too. Frederic even complained that he did not get enough to eat at the school.

The one thing Frederic did like about military school was art class. He had always liked drawing horses. His art notebook was soon filled with pictures of soldiers, battles, and lots of horses.

Turning to Art

Frederic only went to the school in Vermont for one year. Then, he went to the Highland Military Academy in Worcester, Massachusetts. He was a popular and athletic student. He liked to draw **caricatures** of the officers and teachers and show them to other students.

By the time Frederic was 16, his father realized Frederic would never become an army officer. Instead, he was interested in art. Seth and Clara knew that Frederic could draw horses. But, they did not think he was that talented. Still, they let Frederic study what he wanted to.

In 1878, Frederic started classes at the Yale School of the Fine Arts in New Haven, Connecticut. At that time, most art students were girls. Frederic was one of only seven boys in a class of 30 students.

Frederic spent most of his time copying **plaster casts** of **antique** sculptures. However, he hated drawing these **still lifes**. He thought they were boring. He liked drawing people and horses better. Going to Yale was very disappointing for Frederic.

Remington enjoyed sports. He became an important part of Yale's football team. These are drawings he completed while at Yale.

Heading West

Remington's father died of **tuberculosis** in 1880. He was only 46. Remington was very sad. He decided not to return to school. He stayed with his mother for a while. They eventually moved back to Canton to be near other family members.

Remington tried several different jobs in Ogdensburg and Albany, New York. But, he didn't like any of them. In Albany, Remington met Eva Caten. He asked Eva's father if he could marry her. However, her father didn't think Remington would be successful in his life. So he said no.

Remington was very disappointed. He didn't know what he wanted to do with his life. In 1881, Remington decided to go on vacation. He headed west to the Montana Territory. He promised his family he would take a job at an insurance agency when he came back.

Remington saw many exciting things in Montana. He loved the rugged land and the people who lived there. He drew pictures

of Native Americans, soldiers, and cowboys. He drew horses and buffalo. One of his sketches was published by a magazine called *Harper's Weekly*.

Remington knew the West was changing. The railroads were expanding, bringing more people. Soon, the Wild West would disappear. Remington decided to draw pictures of the West so people would remember it when it was gone.

In from the Night Herd *is the type of picture Remington would become famous for. Remington admired the figure of the cowboy all his life.*

Sheep Rancher

Remington's vacation ended too soon. He returned to New York in October and worked at the insurance agency. However, Remington spent more time drawing pictures than working. He soon lost his job.

When he was 21, Remington inherited a lot of money from his father. Now he could go back to the West to make his fortune. Remington moved to Kansas. He bought a sheep ranch with his inheritance money.

However, Remington did not want to work hard to make the ranch succeed. He spent more time boxing, riding **broncos**, and sketching than tending sheep. He was losing money on his investment. Within a year, Remington sold the ranch and returned to Canton.

In March 1884, he moved to Kansas City, Missouri, on another business venture. By August, he had enough money to propose to Eva. They married in Gloversville, New York, on October 1, 1884. Then, the couple moved back to Missouri.

But Eva did not like life in the West. Remington was careless with money and began having financial troubles. She did not like his carefree lifestyle. She did not understand his desire to draw either. Eva only lived in Kansas City with Remington for three months.

Remington stayed in Missouri a while longer. He was able to sell some of his paintings to a local business owner. He also made money publishing sketches in *Harper's Weekly*. By this time, he knew he wanted to be an artist.

Ejecting an "Oklahoma Boomer" *was Remington's second illustration for* Harper's Weekly.

Being an Artist

Remington also knew he needed to learn more about art. In 1885, he moved to New York City to study at a school called the Art Students League. His uncle Bill helped him pay for it. Bill believed art was the career Remington was made for.

Remington became famous almost immediately. In October, he began going to publishing houses looking for a job as an illustrator. *Harper's Weekly* was regularly buying his illustrations. Within a year, he had established himself as a magazine illustrator in New York.

In 1886, *Harper's Weekly* asked Remington to go to Arizona and New Mexico. The magazine wanted him to draw pictures of how the U.S. Army was taking land away from Native Americans. Remington could not wait to get started.

Remington's illustrations and stories about the military campaign appeared in *Harper's Weekly* during the summer of 1886. They were very popular. People wanted to learn more about the American West. They were fascinated with cowboys and horses.

Magazine Illustrations

Remington's illustrations were published in magazines and newspapers before modern printing methods were available. When Remington submitted an image to Harper's Weekly, a wood engraver first had to carve his illustration onto a wood block. Then, the image was printed from the block onto the magazine or newspaper page. The movement and action of Remington's figures were often lost in this transfer. However, people still appreciated his illustrations for their realism.

At first, Remington's style was so rough that Harper's Weekly usually had another artist redraw his sketches.

Fame & Fortune

In his first year as a professional artist, Remington published 25 illustrations and earned $1,200. This was a lot of money in those days. Frederic and Eva had a large apartment in New York City. They lived comfortably there.

In 1887, Remington's paintings were exhibited at several famous art shows. That same year, he created 83 pictures for Theodore Roosevelt's book *Ranch Life*. Sixty-four of the illustrations also appeared in *Century Magazine*.

In 1889, the Remingtons bought a house in New Rochelle, New York. The house had a large studio where Remington could paint. That year, he was also awarded a silver medal at the **Paris Exposition**. By 1890, he was one of America's best-known artists.

Remington illustrated other books, too. He created artwork for *The Song of Hiawatha* by Henry Wadsworth Longfellow. He also wrote his own books and illustrated them. He wrote articles for magazines and newspapers as well.

Artist's Corner

Frederic Remington

Horses were Remington's specialty. But, some people criticized the way he drew horses. His pictures showed horses galloping with all four feet off the ground. Some people said this was not how horses really moved.

However in 1877, a photographer named Eadweard Muybridge had taken a series of photos of a horse galloping. These pictures showed that Remington was right. When a horse gallops, it does have all four feet off the ground at the same time.

Two of the images in the top row of Muybridge's photos (left) show the horse's feet not touching the ground. Remington also often drew his horses this way, as shown in the painting on the right. Because of his reliance on photographs for many of his paintings, Remington was able to draw more realistically.

Bronco Buster

By 1895, Remington had been a professional illustrator and painter for ten years. He wanted to try something new. So, he decided to try sculpture. A friend who was a sculptor helped him practice. Then, Remington went back to his studio.

Remington had a natural talent for sculpting. He began making a sculpture out of clay, mud, and wax. Then, he brought it to a **foundry** in New York City. The foundry **cast** the sculpture in bronze. It was called *The* **Bronco** *Buster.*

The Bronco Buster was exhibited in the window of a famous jewelry store in New York City. *Harper's Weekly* printed pictures of the sculpture and wrote articles about it. *The Bronco Buster* became one of the most famous statues of the American West ever made.

Remington loved sculpting. Like his paintings, Remington's sculptures were full of action. He produced 25 sculptures in the next 14 years. He also continued to paint and draw.

The Bronco Buster *is two feet (1 m) tall.*

At War

In 1898, the United States fought Spain in the **Spanish-American War**. The *New York Journal* sent Remington to Cuba to draw pictures of the soldiers in battle. He was one of their war reporters.

Remington had always been interested in the military. He was the son of a **Civil War** hero. He had also spent time with the army in the West. He liked traveling with the army during wartime. And, he loved to draw military figures in action.

When Remington went to Cuba, he lived just the way the soldiers did. He slept outside, and he marched through the jungle in the rain. However, he was unpopular with the soldiers because he ate too much food.

The war had a great impact on his life. Remington saw the soldiers march into battle. He also saw the soldiers get injured and killed. Seeing war up close made him sad. Many people thought war was an adventure. After traveling with the army, Remington knew this was not true.

During the Spanish-American War, Theodore Roosevelt led a group of soldiers called the Rough Riders. Remington painted this picture called Charge of the Rough Riders at San Juan Hill. *Roosevelt later became president of the United States.*

Remington wanted to let people know what war was really like. He wrote an article about his experience for *Harper's Weekly* in November 1898. He was also asked to create drawings about the war. But, Remington refused. He did not want to remember the horrible things he had seen.

Self-Criticism

In 1900, Remington bought a small island called Ingelneuk. The island was on the St. Lawrence River near Ogdensburg. Remington loved Ingelneuk because it brought him so close to the outdoors. He could be far away from civilization.

In 1905, Remington began making a model of *The Big Cowboy*. This was a huge statue of a cowboy on horseback. It is now located in Fairmount Park in Philadelphia, Pennsylvania. Remington worked on it for several years.

At this same time, his style of painting began to change. He concentrated more on color. He also began painting more landscapes. But, Remington was a harsh judge of his own work. He did not want to save anything that he did not think was the best he could do.

In 1907 and 1908, he burned more than 100 of his old paintings. At the same time, he continued to create new paintings and sculptures. In 1909, an art **critic** said Remington's latest works were among the best he'd ever done.

The Outlier *was painted in 1909.*

A Sudden End

Around 1909, Frederic and Eva built a farmhouse in Ridgefield, Connecticut. However, Remington did not get to enjoy his new home very long. On December 22, 1909, his **appendix** burst. An infection spread throughout his body. On December 26, he died.

Remington left behind almost 3,000 works of art. Eva kept everything until her death nine years later. Then, all of Remington's work was given to the Ogdensburg Public Library. Later, these works became part of the Frederic Remington Art Museum in Ogdensburg.

In a diary entry written in May 1909, Remington claimed he was "performing miracles." He was very happy with his work in the time before his death.

Remington's sculpture *Coming Through the Rye* *at the National
Cowboy and Western Heritage Museum in Oklahoma City*

Today, Remington's art is enjoyed by people all over the world.
His work shows a Wild West that was disappearing even as he
painted it. Through Remington's art, people can relive the days of
the American West and the horses, cowboys, Native Americans,
and soldiers that lived there.

Glossary

antique - an old item that has collectible value.

appendix - an internal organ in the lower right-hand portion of the body, near the intestines.

bronco - a wild horse that has not been trained to wear a saddle.

caricature - a type of cartoonish drawing that makes certain parts of the subject appear bigger and others smaller.

cast - to form into a shape by molding and then separating material from an object.

civil war - a war between groups in the same country. The United States of America and the Confederate States of America fought a civil war from 1861 to 1865.

critic - a professional who gives his or her opinion on art or performances.

discipline - to punish someone as part of the training that teaches order and obedience.

foundry - a place where metals are created.

Paris Exposition - a world fair in Paris, France, that celebrated art and architecture.

plaster cast - a sculptor's model made of paste and water.

Spanish-American War - a war in 1898 between the United States and Spain that ended Spanish rule of Cuba, the Philippines, and other colonies.

still life - a painting or picture made up of nonmoving objects.

tuberculosis - a disease that affects the lungs.

Saying It

Hiawatha - heye-uh-WAW-thuh
Rochelle - ruh-SHEHL
Roosevelt - ROH-zuh-vuhlt
tuberculosis - tu-buhr-kyuh-LOH-suhs
Worcester - WUS-tuhr

Web Sites

To learn more about Frederic Remington, visit ABDO Publishing Company on the World Wide Web at **www.abdopub.com**. Web sites about Remington are featured on our Book Links page. These links are routinely monitored and updated to provide the most current information available.

Index